Throwing Techniques

Joaquim Chavarria

WATSON-GUPTILL PUBLICATIONS/NEW YORK

Ceramics Class: Throwing Techniques
Original Spanish title:
  Aula de cerámica: Torno
Editorial director: María Fernanda Canal
Text and exercises: Joaquim Chavarria
Graphic Design: Carlos Bonet
Diagrams: SET. Seveis Editorials i Tècnics
Dummy: Pedro González
Photography: Nos & Soto
Archive research: Mª Carmen Ramos
Translation: Mark Lodge

First published in the United States in 1999 by Watson-Guptill
Publications, a division of BPI Communications, Inc.
1515 Broadway, New York, N.Y. 10036

Copyright ©1998 Parramón Ediciones, S.A.
Gran Via de les Corts Catalanes, 322-324
08004 Barcelona, Spain

Library of Congress Catalog Card Number: 98-83064
ISBN 0-8230-0593-3

Manufactured in Spain

1 2 3 4 5 / 03 02 01 00 99

CONTENTS

INTRODUCTION

The potter's wheel has existed since about 3500 B.C. First used in Mesopotamia, it was later adopted by cultures in Asia Minor and Egypt. In the second millennium B.C. the invention reached Crete, followed by Greece. It became known in Italy toward the seventh century B.C. It was evidently used in China during the Han Dynasty (1206 B.C. to A.D. 220) and from there it spread to Korea and Japan.

Not only did the wheel allow ancient potters to make pieces more quickly, it also gave them the opportunity to experiment with more plastic types of clay that were better suited to the wheel. At the same time it enabled them to vary the shapes somewhat, though the results would always be round.

For those new to the medium it is best to work with simple forms. At first the machine and the clay body spinning on the wheelhead take over and it may seem impossible to achieve the desired results. Only with practice can this shapeless mass be converted into a hollow, symmetrical piece in which convex and concave forms, contour and surface unite to form a harmonious whole.

The throwing technique generally entails two processes: throwing the piece itself, and then turning it. The first process involves creating a piece from a lump of well-kneaded clay or other ceramic body by placing it on a wheel that is rotating at a particular speed. This first process can be divided into four stages:

1. Centering the clay on the wheelhead
2. Opening the lump
3. Raising the walls
4. Shaping the piece

Turning is a continuation of the previous process, although not all thrown pieces will need to be turned. In this phase, any excess clay or ceramic body is removed, lending the walls a more uniform thickness and finishing off the shape of the piece. For this operation, the piece must be in a leather-hard state of dryness. The next steps are drying and firing the piece.

This book provides the necessary background and instructions to start beginners on their way to carrying on the age-old craft of pottery making. Professionals use methods somewhat similar to those described here; although each potter's technique is very personal, there are many basic processes used by all potters.

Throwing pieces on a wheel may seem deceptively simple when observing an experienced potter at work. But beginners should not be daunted by the difficulties they may encounter early on. The manual skills required are fairly straightforward and anyone can learn them; the process is not especially demanding but it must be practiced methodically. The most fundamental element is to learn to place the hands and fingers correctly on the clay or other ceramic body. Above all the art of throwing requires a great deal of serenity and patience, qualities essential not only for acquiring sufficient skill to enjoy a newly learned craft, but also for attaining personal and artistic enrichment.

To all of you, my best wishes.

Joaquim-Manuel Chavarria Climent

THE POTTER'S WHEEL

The earliest potters created their pieces with the coil and pinch techniques. The invention of the potter's wheel was a significant advance, enabling a whole new approach to the use of clay.

The ancient potter's wheel consisted of a stone or a piece of wood (the base on which the clay was placed) affixed to the end of a rotating axle (the pivot) whose other end was stuck into the ground. The first wheels were turned with the hands, and later with the feet.

The wheel slowly changed over a long period, evolving from the heavy stone wheel to the lighter wooden one, increasing in efficiency with each change. Some wheels required two people to operate: the potter who threw the pieces and an assistant who moved the wheel by turning a flywheel. Some potters today, particularly in North Africa, still use a potter's wheel placed in a hole dug into the floor of the workshop. To throw, the potter sits at the edge of the

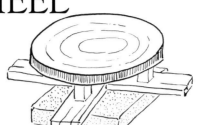

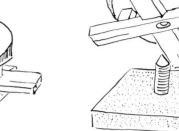

hole and pushes a flywheel with the feet.

Nowadays several different types of potter's wheel are used, both manual and mechanical, operating through the use of pedals, flywheels, or electricity. Pedal-operated

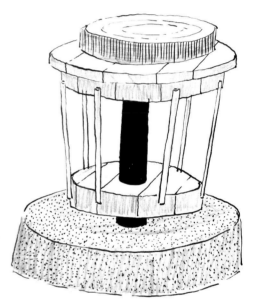

Two manual potter's wheels used to throw large pots.

The foot-operated potter's wheel.

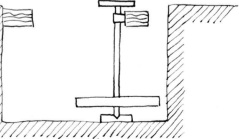

A potter's wheel in a pit that I encountered in a potter's workshop in Nabeul (Tunisia) in 1986.

wheels are turned by means of a pedal pushed with one foot; thus the lower body is in constant motion while the upper body must remain still for throwing, a condition that can cause difficulties during the learning stage. This type of wheel is rarely used today.

The flywheel-operated potter's wheel is so called because it is made of a strong wooden or metal frame containing a heavy flywheel that is moved by the foot, causing the wheelhead to rotate. This type of wheel consists of a vertical axle or tree. The potter sits on a slightly slanted seat and rests the left foot on a crossbar above the flywheel, not touching it. The flywheel is put into motion and throwing begins, continuing until the wheelhead begins to lose speed. At first it is difficult to push with the foot and throw at the same time, but with practice this becomes easy. Small to medium-sized pieces can be thrown with this wheel, but large pieces are more difficult.

The electric potter's wheel is smaller and lighter than the flywheel-operated type. It runs on an electric motor that can reach a speed of up to 240 revolutions per minute. The velocity-control

mechanism can be operated by hand or by foot. Pieces of any size can be thrown on this wheel as long as the motor is potent enough. The great advantage of the electric wheel is that it allows the potter to concentrate on the movements of the hands without having to worry about anything else, so all energy can be directed toward throwing without having to worry about working the wheel itself.

Nowadays the electric potter's wheel is essential for throwing. It occupies little space and is very versatile.

TOOLS

Throwing ribs. Made of metal, wood, rubber, or hard plastic, these tools are used to smooth the surface of a piece when throwing on the wheel. Thanks to the variety of shapes available, they are often useful in the creation process itself. The metallic ones are also used during turning.

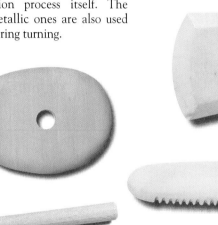

Throwing ribs

Bats

Cutting wire. Made of steel or nylon, this is used to cut clay and to remove pieces from the wheelhead. Rings or handles at the ends provide grip and make it easy to handle without injuring yourself.

Bats. Round and flat in form, about 3/4 inch (2 cm) thick and of varying diameter, these disks are placed on the wheelhead to provide a larger surface for bigger pieces, or support for pieces that should not be removed from the surface immediately after throwing.

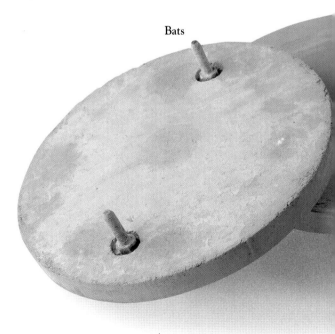

Cutting wires

Compass or calipers. Used for tracing circumferences and for measuring distances, this instrument consists of two long pieces joined together at one end. Made of metal, wood, or plastic, they come in different shapes according to their function. The straight-armed ones are used for measuring height, the curved ones for width. Some are equipped with a little screw tightener to set a measurement when working on a series of the same type of pots.

Turning tools. This tool consists of a wooden handle with a rectangular, triangular, or rounded head made of metal. The beveled edge of the head is applied to the surface of the piece to remove excess clay.

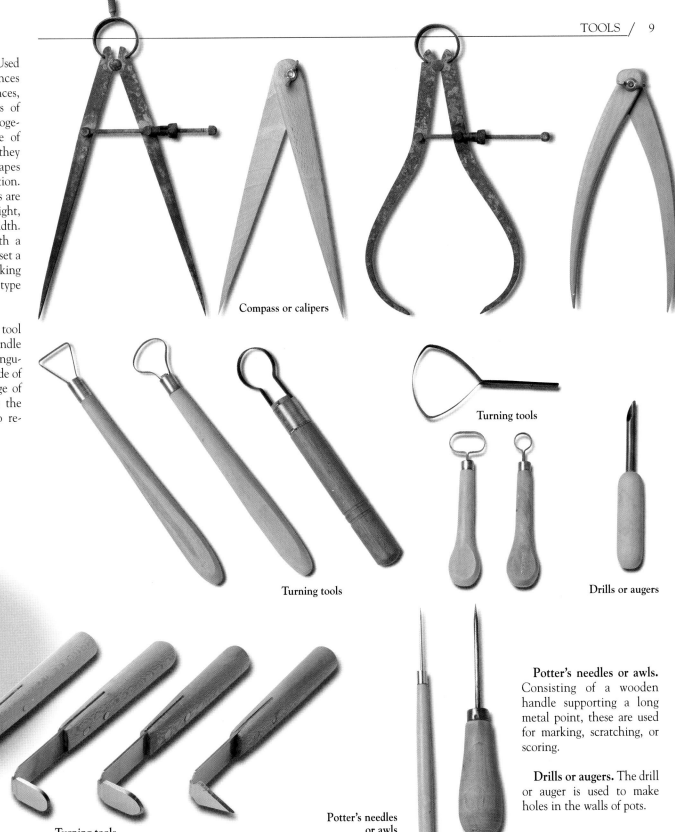

Compass or calipers

Turning tools

Turning tools

Drills or augers

Turning tools

Potter's needles or awls

Potter's needles or awls. Consisting of a wooden handle supporting a long metal point, these are used for marking, scratching, or scoring.

Drills or augers. The drill or auger is used to make holes in the walls of pots.

MATERIALS

Pieces thrown on a wheel require a very plastic ceramic body that can hold a shape without weakening or falling apart. Certain clays can be used in their natural state, with the addition of water; other clays must be combined with additional materials. Early potters had to prepare their own clay mixtures for throwing, but nowadays commercially prepared clay is widely available in a variety of mixtures. Sometimes grog clay that is bisque-fired and ground up coarsely or finely is added to clay to prevent thick pieces from cracking or thin pieces from warping. Clay containing grog is sometimes known as raku.

In addition to purchasing commercial preparations, today's potters can learn to create their own ceramic body by mixing the appropriate components. Although the process takes practice and careful attention to detail, there are advantages to mixing your own ceramic body, which allows you to tailor the clay to your specific needs. Once you become more proficient on the wheel and have experimented with

various types of clay, you may wish to explore preparing your own clay.

The different types of clay bodies used in the basic exercises in this book are stoneware for the bowl, white earthenware for the plate, stoneware with fine grog for the cylindrical pot, and red earthenware for the vase.

Types of Ceramic Body

Stoneware. Stoneware is nonporous, vitreous, and opaque after firing. Firing temperatures range from 2102 to 2372°F (1150 to 1300°C). The resulting color may be gray, ivory, beige, or brown, among others. Stoneware may contain grog.

White earthenware. White earthenware is a porous white or ivory-colored clay that requires a final glazing after the initial firing. There are three different kinds: hard, mixed, and soft.

The hard type is bisque-fired at a temperature between 2156 and 2372°F (1180 to 1300°C) and vitrifies at 1922 to 2156°F (1050 to 1180°C).

The mixed type is bisque-fired at 1922 to 2156°F (1050 to 1180°C) and vitrifies at 1832 to 2012°F (1000 to 1100°C). The soft type is bisque-fired at 1760 to 1976°F (960 to 1080°C) and vitrifies at the same temperatures.

Red earthenware. Red earthenware gets its color from the high iron content. Firing temperatures range from 1742 to 2012°F (950 to 1100°C). The great plasticity of this clay makes it well suited to modeling and throwing.

a. Stoneware with coarse grog
b. Stoneware
c. Stoneware with fine grog
d. Red earthenware
e. White earthenware
f. Gray earthenware

PLASTICITY AND SHRINKAGE

The plasticity of a ceramic body is what allows it to keep the shape given to it in throwing. Plasticity would not exist without water, since the particles of clay would not be able to slide over each other. The degree of plasticity also depends on the size of the particles. Very plastic clays absorb much water and increase in volume, but when too much water is absorbed plasticity decreases and the clay becomes a soft, pasty mass due to the loss of adherence capacity of the clay particles. Clays containing an excess of water must be allowed to lose some of their moisture before they can be used.

After preparing a ceramic paste, it is essential to let it rest for a time, keeping it covered to prevent it from losing its moisture content. Aging makes clays and pastes more plastic and easier to knead.

To test the plasticity of clay or ceramic body, roll a small piece into a ball and then roll the ball out to form a coil (a long snakelike shape). Make an arch with the coil. If the clay cracks when bent into an arch, it has a low degree of plasticity and will be difficult to work. To eliminate the problem, mix it with another, more plastic clay.

1. Examining a coil shaped into an arch reveals the clay's plasticity. The smooth surfaces and absence of cracks here indicate that these clays are sufficiently plastic for throwing.

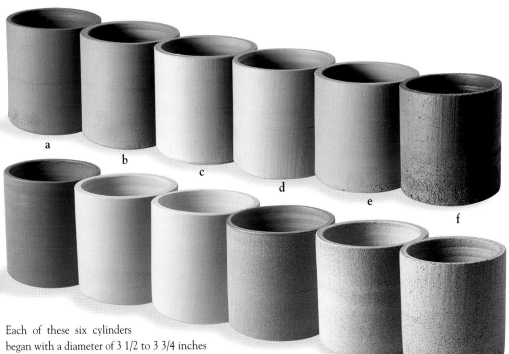

Shrinkage

Moist clay and ceramic bodies become harder in contact with air and their volume decreases as they dry. Drying occurs by capillary action, so that as the surface dries, the water in the interior is sucked toward the surface, evaporating little by little. Called shrinkage or contraction, the process happens because the particles of clay come closer together as they lose water. Shrinkage depends both on the size of the particles and on the quantity of water separating them. Clays that absorb much water will shrink more than less plastic ones. Clays with finer particles will shrink more than those with larger particles. The introduction of nonplastic materials into a clay body speeds up the drying process, since these materials absorb less water.

Shrinkage occurs not only during drying but also during firing. Pieces dried at room temperature will still contain some moisture, which is eliminated during the early firing stage, as the kiln reaches 212°F (100°C), the boiling point of water.

Only then can they be considered dry. The water evaporating at this early stage forms part of the physical composition of clay, whereas the water forming part of the chemical composition of clay will disappear at 1022°F (550°C). At this temperature a chemical reaction takes place that irreversibly changes the structure of the clay body, making it hard and compact.

Each of these six cylinders began with a diameter of 3 1/2 to 3 3/4 inches (9 to 9.5 cm) and a height of 4 inches (10 cm). After each was thrown it was allowed to dry and then fired, the earthenware at 1832°F (1000°C) and the stoneware at 2282°F (1250°C). As a result of shrinkage, the resulting sizes vary as follows:

a. Red earthenware: 3 1/8 x 3 1/2 in.
b. White earthenware: 3 3/8 x 3 9/16 in.
c. White earthenware: 3 7/16 x 3 11/16 in.
d. Buff stoneware: 3 1/8 x 3 5/16 in.
e. Stoneware with fine grog: 3 3/16 x 3 7/16 in.
f. Stoneware with coarse grog: 3 1/4 x 3 9/16 in.

KNEADING THE CLAY

The earliest potters created their pieces with the coil and pinch techniques. The invention of the potter's wheel was a significant advance, since it enabled a whole new approach to the use of clay.

The ancient potter's wheel consisted of a stone or a piece of wood (the base on which the clay was placed) affixed to the end of a rotating axle (the pivot) whose other end was stuck into the ground. The first wheels

were turned with the hands, and later with the feet.

The wheel slowly changed over a long period, evolving from the heavy stone wheel to the lighter wooden one, increasing in efficiency with each change. Some wheels

required two people to operate: the potter who threw the pieces and an assistant who moved the wheel by turning a flywheel. Some potters today, particularly in North Africa, still use a potter's wheel placed in a hole

dug into the floor of the workshop. To throw, the potter sits at the edge of the hole and pushes a flywheel with the feet.

Nowadays several different types of potter's wheel are used, both manual and

Basic Kneading Technique

1. Cut a piece of clay and place it on the board, pressing with both hands as if kneading dough to form a roll.

2. As the clay becomes more elongated, bring your hands closer together, pressing hard with the palms. Twist your hands in opposite directions to divide the roll in half.

3. Once the clay is divided, check for any poorly kneaded areas, which will show up as cavities. Place one roll in each hand and extend your arms so your hands are far apart, preparing to bang them together.

4. Slam the two parts together with force, so they begin to meld together.

5. Place the elongated piece of clay perpendicular to the work surface and begin kneading again.

6. Knead the clay again until both parts become entirely fused, repeating the process as many times as necessary until the clay mass has reached a homogenous consistency.

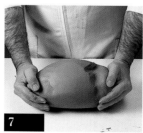

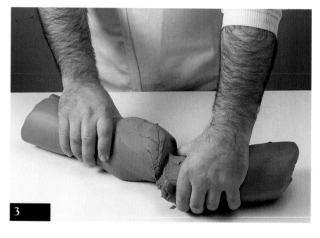

7. Take the clay in both hands and beat it against the table repeatedly so that the clay bounces back. In between each impact, roll it in your hands. The impacts cause the clay to compact and the rolling motion rounds it off.

8. Continue beating and rolling the clay until a cylinder is formed.

9. A properly kneaded cylinder of clay will look something like this.

mechanical, operating through the use of pedals, flywheels, or electricity. Pedal-operated wheels are turned by means of a pedal pushed with one foot; thus the lower body is in constant motion while the upper body must remain still for throwing, a condition that can cause difficulties during the learning stage. This type of wheel is rarely used today. The flywheel-operated potter's wheel is so called because it is made of a strong wooden or metal frame containing a heavy flywheel that is moved by the foot, causing the wheelhead to rotate. This type of wheel consists of a vertical axle or tree. The potter sits on a slightly slanted seat and rests the left foot on a crossbar above the fly wheel, not touching it. The flywheel is put into motion and throwing begins, continuing until the wheelhead begins to lose speed. At first it is difficult to push with the foot and throw at the same time, but with practice is becomes easy. Small to medium-sized pieces can be thrown with this wheel, but large pieces are more difficult.

The electric potter's wheel is smaller and lighter than the flywheel-operated type. It runs on an electric motor that can reach a speed of up to 240 revolutions per minute. The velocity-control mechanism can be operated by hand or by foot. Pieces of any size can be thrown on this wheel as long as the motor is potent enough. The great advantage of the electric wheel is that it allows the potter to concentrate on the movements of the hands without having to worry about anything else, so all energy can be directed toward throwing without having to worry about working the wheel itself.

Spiral-Wedge Technique

10. The spiral-wedge method relies on the weight of the entire body when pushing down the clay. The clay is rotated with the left hand; it rises toward the right hand, which is used to push it back down.

11. Lift the clay in the left hand, twist it, and push down with the right hand.
This process involves oscillating as well as rotating movements.

12. Rhythmically repeat the lifting, twisting, pushing action.

13. Note that the clay begins to form a spiral.

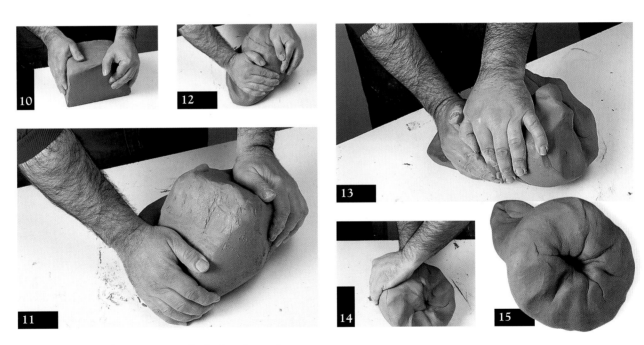

Continue repeating the movement to slowly close the spiral.
A small cavity will form in the center but will disappear as the kneading continues.

14. Lift the clay mass and continue to knead in the same way. Note the placement of the hands when closing the spiral.

15. The cavity seen in the center of the spiral will disappear as the kneading continues.

16. Continue with the same movement, raising the clay with the left hand and pushing it down with the right. As kneading progresses, a cone shape will slowly form. Exert downward pressure with the palm of the right hand, while holding the other part of the clay with the left hand. The left hand keeps the clay balanced as the right moves forward.

17. Once the cone has been formed, beat it against the table, trying to maintain the shape while making it more compact.

18. When correctly done, the kneaded clay will look something like this.

THE ROLE OF THE HANDS

Throwing pieces on the wheel involves a series of movements and positioning of the hands in order to transform a lump of clay or other ceramic body into a bowl, plate, cylindrical vase, or jug, the basic forms on which all pieces are based. Practice with each piece repeatedly before moving on to the next shape, and try to eliminate any bad habits now, since they will be much more difficult to get rid of later.

The techniques are fairly simple, but they do require time and patience. The movements and positions must be practiced enough that they become automatic. The following exercises demonstrate how to use the hands to create all the pieces in this book. The movements suggested should be taken only as a guide for getting started. With experience, each person will find his or her own personal method.

The hands and fingers should have minimal contact with the clay, and what contact there is should consist of controlled movements and positions; avoid brusque gestures. Except in larger pieces, the hands should always be held together, forming a single unit, so that the throwing process is controlled.

Different parts of the hands are used for different aspects of throwing. The base of the palm is used to press the clay into its centered position on the wheelhead, as well as to flatten it when shaping the inside bottom part of the plate. The hollow center of the palm is also used to press the lump of clay into the wheelhead when centering it. The side of the hand serves to push the mass of clay toward the center during the centering process, as well as to model the exterior wall when throwing plates and cylindrical pots.

The thumb can be used to model the upper part of the lump of clay during centering, to open it up and to pinch, along with the index finger, when controlling the rim of the piece and tracing the cutting line, as well as to keep the hands together. The interior of a piece can be smoothed with the tip of the thumb.

The index finger is used to widen an opening made with the thumb. It also makes the walls rise and become thinner. Pressure is applied on the clay and modeling is carried out with the fingertips, which also serve to control the rim.

The walls of a bowl can be thinned by pinching between the middle finger and the thumb. The base of the palm is used to raise and thin the lump of clay after centering. For larger pieces, the closed fist can be used to widen a piece from the interior, controlling the pressure exerted by resting the wrist of that hand on the palm of the other. With the knuckles of the index finger, the ceramic body is drawn upward and the walls of the piece are thinned.

These tasks are the same for both hands. Thus, left-handed people should perform the same tasks with the left hand, making sure to change the direction of rotation of the wheelhead so that it turns clockwise. For right-handers, the wheelhead should rotate in a counterclockwise direction.

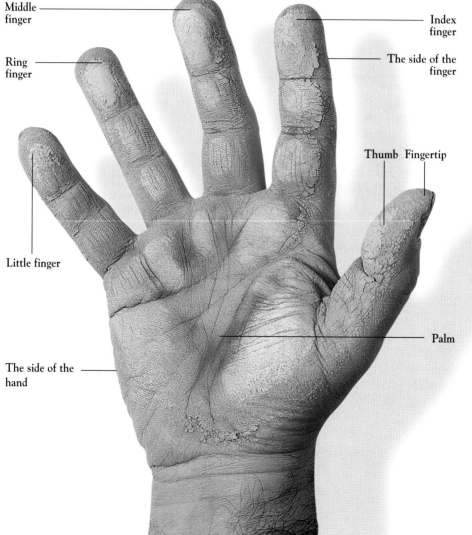

Middle finger

Ring finger

Little finger

The side of the hand

Index finger

The side of the finger

Thumb Fingertip

Palm

BASIC EXERCISES

*O*ne of the most basic operations in making any piece is centering, which consists of a series of movements with the hands and fingers that serve to center the lump of clay on the wheelhead. It is the most important operation, since it will determine whether the final piece is good or bad. Other operations follow this, such as raising and thinning a cone, opening the lump, raising the walls, and shaping the piece. All these procedures are demonstrated on the following pages. The clay used for this exercise is red earthenware.

Centering, Lowering, and Raising

1. Place the lump of clay on the wheelhead and moisten both it and your hands.

2. With your right hand, push the clay mass downward. With your left hand, hold the mass steady to counterbalance the pressure exerted by the right and at the same time, push toward the center of the wheelhead.

3. As the clay moves downward, it becomes more compact. With your right hand open you can better control the cone and continue to apply pressure. The left hand should remain in the previous position, pushing toward the center.

4. Place both hands on the base of the cone so that the lower palms are touching the very outer edge of the cone.

5. Pressing with the base of your palms, draw the cone upward, making sure to keep it centered.

6. Place your right palm on top of the cone, with your left hand next to it on the side. As you push downward with the right hand, counterbalance with the left to keep the cone steady. Slowly lower both hands at the same time to continue centering.

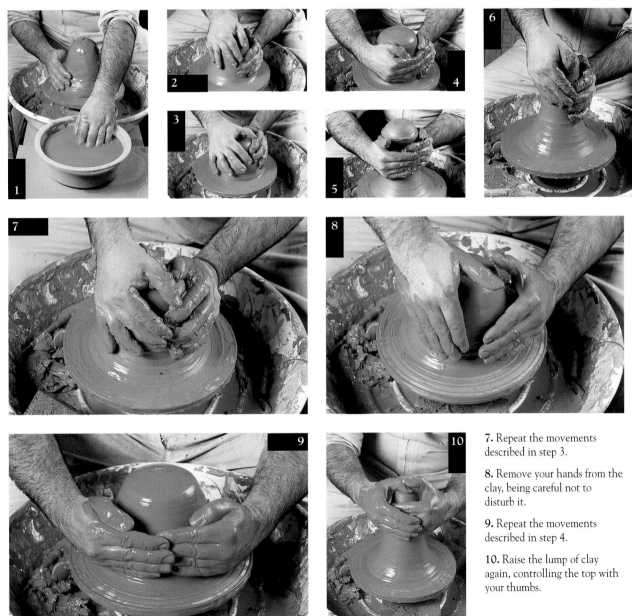

7. Repeat the movements described in step 3.

8. Remove your hands from the clay, being careful not to disturb it.

9. Repeat the movements described in step 4.

10. Raise the lump of clay again, controlling the top with your thumbs.

Cutting

11. Continue to draw the cone upward while making it thinner, until it has reached the desired height. With your left thumb, make an incision to mark the cutting line.

12. With a cutting wire that has a wooden stick tied to the end, cut the clay along the marked line by wetting the cutting wire and positioning it over the wheelhead, stretching it taut with the other hand.

13. Let the cutting wire move slowly up the side of the cone, trying to avoid getting it caught and cutting the clay in the wrong place. This step should be repeated as many times as necessary. At first it will probably get caught in the clay and cut into it, making it necessary to repeat the entire process of centering and raising the cone.

14. Let the cutting wire reach the cutting line traced with the thumb.

15. When the cutting wire reaches the correct point, allow it to slice into the clay to make a clean cut. Keep the cutting wire taut so the cut part of the cone remains in place. It is important to keep the wheelhead spinning steadily, so that a sudden change in centrifugal force does not cause the piece to move.

16. This cutting method is used with pieces made of a single lump of clay. Various cuts are seen here, along with a demonstration of cutting the base of a small jar.

17. Other methods are used to even a defective or warped rim. One of these consists of taking a nylon cutting wire in both hands and placing it over the rim.

18. With the wheelhead turning, hold the cutting wire taut and let it cut into the piece about 3/8 inch (1 cm) down from the top.

19. Without stopping the wheel, pull the cutting wire upward to remove the cut part.

Lips to Hold Lids

The lip that holds a lid on a piece is normally made with the fingers or with a rib.

20. Place the index finger and thumb of your left hand on the inside rim of the piece. Bend your right index finger and place it and your right thumb on the outside of the rim.

21. With the right hand, model the outer rim while carefully pushing downward with the left, forming a lip.

22. Take a rectangular rib in your right hand and rest it on your left thumb. The rib should be placed in the middle of the rim.

23. Push downward with the rib to finish off the lip. Meanwhile, to avoid warping, control the rim and the exterior with the left index and middle fingers.

Throwing a Pot with the Coil Method

A pot can also be thrown using the coil technique. This exercise uses stoneware clay with coarse grog, so it's best to wear plastic gloves and continually lubricate them in slip.

1. Center a kneaded lump of clay on the wheelhead.

2. Open the lump, pulling outward with the left hand while controlling the pressure with the right.

3. With the rectangular rib, clean and smooth the inner base.

4. Prepare coils from the same clay, about 3/4 inch (2 cm) in diameter. Place one on the thrown base.

5. Cut off the excess of the coil at an oblique angle, leaving it long enough to overlap somewhat to provide for a strong joint, and press the ends together with the thumb.

6. With the wheelhead spinning, quickly smooth over the top of the coil with the fingertips. Place another coil on the first and carry out the same procedure. After adding several more rolls, smooth off the exterior with a rectangular rib.

7. Cut off the top of the rim with a needle in order to make it even.

8. Continue adding coils until the pot has reached the desired height.

9. With two turns of the wheel, widen the pot with the knuckles of your right fist, and then smooth the rim by pinching it between your fingers. The piece is finished. If you want to continue building the pot higher, wait an hour or two until the thrown clay becomes harder so it can support the next layers.

Turning Thrown Pieces

Turning entails removing any extra ceramic body that remains after throwing. This extra clay generally accumulates at the bottom of the pot and should be eliminated in order to achieve the most uniform wall thickness possible. Turning should be done when a piece has reached the leather-hard state during drying. It is impossible to turn a piece when it is in a softer state, and also quite difficult when it is harder since the tools are specifically designed for scraping off clay in the leather-hard state.

Pieces can be turned either right side up or upside down, with a chuck or with the piece placed directly on the wheelhead. The latter option has several drawbacks. The piece must be supported with a roll of clay, which adds moisture. If the piece is high, it is difficult to keep in place and comes easily off center. If the neck is long, the piece cannot be turned without a chuck.

Some wheelheads come with a mechanical anchoring device to hold the piece in place. Some ceramists even use prefabricated chucks made of plaster or bisque-fired clay, but this requires having many different chucks on hand to fit the different shapes.

For turning, I suggest making a chuck on the wheel, a process that can be carried out quickly. Some advantages are that it fits the piece perfectly and can be easily redone during turning. It can be adapted to various pieces with minimal changes and gives the greatest stability. Also, it can be prepared in proportion to the piece to be turned. With practice, you will be able to decide for yourself which system works best for you.

Tools should be held firmly during turning. The hand holding the tool should rest on the other hand, and the arms should rest against the sides of the body to form a compact unit. The tool should touch the piece at an angle and should not dig in too deeply. The shape of the inside serves as the guide for the clay to be removed from the outside.

The following exercises explain all the procedures involved in turning.

THROWING A BOWL

This is the easiest exercise for learning to throw a bowl. You should memorize all the hand positions needed. The basic hand movements are centering the clay, opening it, forming the basic shape of the bowl, controlling the rim, marking out the base, shaping and finishing, second control of the rim, and cutting the bowl from the main body of clay. The centrifugal force of the potter's wheel helps to achieve the open form of the bowl. These bowls are made of a mixture of different types of stoneware. A bat has been placed over the wheelhead to allow the bowl to be handled without the danger of deforming it after it has been thrown.

1. Using both hands, throw the lump of clay down hard onto the wheelhead, situating it as centrally as possible on the wheel. Then wet both the lump and your hands.

2. Exert pressure with the right hand, from top to bottom, and with the left hand press into the center of the clay. Repeat the procedure and draw the cone of clay upward.

3. When the cone has reached the right height, without moving your hands place your thumbs at the top of the cone in order to center it on the wheelhead. With the thumbs held parallel to each other, regulate the upper part of the cone.

4. Start to open the bowl. Raise your left thumb without

moving the rest of your hand, which should stay in the same position.

5. With the cone now open, throw some water into it to keep it lubricated.

6. Open out the bowl shape, drawing up the required amount of clay for the shape you want. Then place the right index finger and left thumb on the inside, at an angle, and push toward the center to open up the clay. Note how both hands are used to control the cone on the outside.

7. With the thumbnail, mark out where the base of the bowl will be.

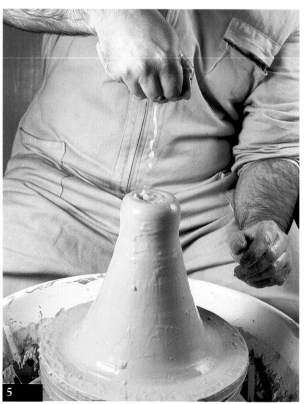

8. Begin to shape the bowl. Link the thumb and middle finger of the right hand, placing the index finger inside the bowl, and let the clay slip between the three fingers. At the same time, place the left hand around the bowl, but with the index finger resting on the rim to keep it centered. The thumb of this hand is linked with the right hand, so that both hands are controlling the pot with the thumbs kept stationary.

9. In the same position, and without moving the left hand, start to raise the right hand, exerting pressure with the three fingers so that the bowl gets thinner and taller.

10. Make a pincer shape with the index finger and thumb of the left hand, and with the side of the right finger control the rim of the bowl to keep it centered.

11. Place all the fingers of the left hand inside the bowl. Bend the fingers of the right hand so that the thumb and index finger touch, and put the left thumb in the hollow between the two.

12. Repeat position 10 to regulate the rim of the piece. The bowl is now complete.

13. With a damp, squeezed-out sponge, soak up the water that has collected inside the bowl.

14. It is time to cut the clay with a fine silk wire. Control the wire with the right hand and hold the other end between the left thumb and index finger, keeping it taut.

15. With the wheel turning, let go of the left end that falls onto the wheelhead; this motion takes the wire with it. With the right hand, draw up the cone wall. It is essential to keep your hand and the wire parallel to the wheelhead.

16. The wire has reached the incision made with the thumbnail to mark the base. Let it cut into the clay, cutting off the bowl at the base. Pull the wire. The bowl keeps revolving as if it were still attached.

17. Clean your hands and position them as shown in the photograph, with the wheel still turning.

18. Grasp the bowl very lightly with the thumb and first two fingertips of each hand, and push upward to remove it from the cone. (The wheel's motion should make it easier.) Note the clean cut at the top of the cone. You can now make another, bigger bowl with the remaining cone. Begin with the same procedure as the first bowl, but in the second open position. Insert your thumbs to draw the clay outward.

19. Place all the fingers of both hands inside the cone. Note that the hands are linked in order to keep the piece centered.

20. With the fingers of the left hand (but not the thumb, which should touch the bottom of the right palm outside the bowl), push with the left hand to open the bowl more. Hence, the left hand pushes outward while the right controls the pressure being exerted.

21. To regulate the edge of the cylinder, make a pincer with the right index and middle fingers over the rim, while the left index finger keeps the upper part firm. The thumbs should be in contact with the bottom part.

22. The right hand should be slightly clenched, the index finger bent together with the thumb, with the left thumb on top of them. Let the clay slip between them and the right index finger placed inside the piece.

23. In order to keep the bowl centered, when you reach the top, stop the movement before removing your hands.

24. Control the rim of the bowl, making the clay slip between the right index finger and the middle fingers and thumb.

25. Using a semicircular rib, round off the outer part of the bowl. Hold the tool between the right hand against the left thumb. It is now time to give the bowl its definitive shape.

26. Still in the same position as the previous step, the clay slips between the rib and the index finger of the left hand, which exerts pressure from inside the bowl. Note that the rib is still held in the right hand and supported by the left thumb. Once this step is finished, make a pincer with the left index finger and thumb, and with the corner of the index finger, control the rim to ensure it remains centered.

27. Use the rib to clean the surface of the bat as well as the perimeter of the bowl base. Turn off the wheel and cut the bowl at the base using a nylon wire. Remove the bat from the wheel. Let the bowl harden without touching it, until it is time to smooth it down. Work with pieces on the bat to avoid tiny deformations that can arise when removing it with the hands.

28. To begin forming a foot on the bowl, prepare a lump of clay for the chuck and center it on the wheel, giving it a truncated conical shape, open at the top, with a diameter less than that of the bowl.

29. With the wheel switched off, grasp the bowl with both hands and check to be sure the support piece is the right size.

30. Place several clean cotton cloths around the piece so it does not stick to the bowl.

31. Overlap the cloths in the same direction as the wheel turns, otherwise they will be pulled off as the wheel spins. The rags prevent the piece from sticking to the chuck and allow it to be moved more easily.

32. With the wheel turned on, carefully turn the bowl over the chuck, pressing gently at intervals until the bowl is centered.

33. Using a potter's needle and supporting it against the opposite thumb, mark out a circumference on the bowl base; this will help indicate that the bowl has been centered.

34. Run a round modeling tool around the edge to remove excess clay from the surface of the base.

35. Continue rounding off the outer surface of the bowl, running the tool from the base to the mouth.

36. Use the rectangular rib to press into the base and start to shape the outside of the base.

37. Use a modeling tool to remove thin shavings of clay. Note the position of the left thumb, which should be in constant contact with the tool.

38. Using a semicircular rib, round off the outer part of the base.

39. With the triangular modeling tool, make a bevel around the outer edge.

40. Using the same tool, make an incision on the inner part of the base.

41. Continue working on the inner part, removing excess clay. Note how the left hand holds the bowl and the left thumb helps support the tool.

42. With a round rib, round off the inner part of the base.

43. Using the same tool, cut a bevel in the top part of the inner rim.

44. Run the semicircular rib over the flat surface of the bowl to smoothe it over and give it sheen.

45. The finished product should look something like this.

46. With clean, dry hands, carefully remove the bowl from the chuck, trying not to spoil its shape. Allow it to dry on a wooden board.

THROWING A PLATE

*W*hen throwing plates, it's best to use a wooden bat on the wheelhead to remove the finished piece without disturbing it. There are two ways to secure these bats to the wheelhead. One is to make two holes in the wheelhead to fit the two anchoring pieces that come on some bats, and the other is to center a ring of clay on the wheelhead on which to stick the bat.

This exercise uses the latter method, with white earthenware.

1. Prepare the ring of clay that will serve to anchor the bat on the wheelhead. After kneading it, center the earthenware by pressing with the base of your palms. Once it is centered, cross the thumbs over each other and press them into the middle to create a slightly concave shape.

2. Place your left index, middle, and ring fingers and your right index finger in the hollow and press inward to open the clay, while your right thumb rests on your left hand to steady it and push it down. Shape the clay with your left pinkie and right middle, ring, and pinkie fingers. Keeping your right hand in the same position and moving your left thumb in the hollow, pull outward to widen the opening and begin forming the ring.

3. Pinch the clay between your left thumb and index finger

while your right hand holds the ring. Note how both hands remain closely united to avoid shifting the ring off center.

4. Holding your hands in the same position, slowly widen the ring until it reaches the diameter of the bat.

5. With the wheelhead on slow speed, center the bat, holding it in both hands.

6. Once the bat is centered, pound it in the very center with your fist to attach it well. The air trapped in the ring will create a suction that will hold the bat in place.

7. When the disc is in place, add the prepared lump of clay for the plate and center it, pressing with the base of your palms. Once it is centered, cross your thumbs over the top.

8. Using both thumbs, open the clay until it is ready for the next step.

9. Change the position of your right hand, placing your index, middle, and ring fingers on the inside of the opening along with your left thumb and push down to widen the opening. Your right thumb should be pushing on your left hand, and you should control the outer wall with the left fingers.

10. Begin to form the base of the plate without letting it come off center, pulling outward with your hands in the same position. As the base widens, remove your right fingers one by one until only the index finger remains.

11. Pinch the clay between your left thumb and index finger to thin it while your right hand maintains the shape. Note that your left thumb should rest on the base of your right palm. As with the bowl, pull upward, making the clay pass between your bent left index finger, the right index finger, and both thumbs.

12. Use the rectangular rib to smooth the inner base of the plate, uniting your hands as shown here.

13. With the same rib, smooth the outer wall of the plate, which is still in a bowl shape.

14. Form a unit by touching your right thumb and middle finger, and let the clay pass between this unit and your right index finger. Control the rim with your left index finger. Your thumbs should be touching each other.

15. Pinch the rim between your left index finger and thumb, and level it with the side of your right index finger.

16. Holding the wall between your left index finger and your right thumb and index finger, begin to shape the plate by pulling outward.

17. Continue in the same position, but now push downward with your left fingers to begin flattening the wall.

18. With a moist, wrung-out sponge, clean the interior of the plate as the wheelhead is turning.

19. The throwing stage is finished. Stretch a nylon cutting wire taut, place it on the bat, and slide it under the plate to detach it. Note that the thumbs are as close as possible to the base of the plate. This will help you keep a grip on the cutting wire as you cut and avoid cutting up into the plate and making the base weak and thin. Remove the bat from the wheelhead and leave the plate on it to harden undisturbed.

20 to 25. When the plate is leather-hard, it should be turned. As with bowls, this

should always be done with the piece face down, since the inside was already finished during throwing. If you are using a chuck (which is recommended), it should be fitted to the middle part of the inside, leaving the edge of the plate free to avoid having it crack or warp from excess pressure. Prepare a chuck of the appropriate size by opening the clay as if beginning another plate. Push on the center of the clay lump with your left fingers and right thumb while your left thumb rests on the back of your right hand. At the same time, your four right fingers should hold the chuck from the outside. Deepen the opening with your hands in the same position, pulling outward to open it to the right size.

26. Clean the inside of the chuck out with a damp sponge.

27. With the wheel at a standstill, check to see if the plate fits on the chuck.

28. Cover the chuck with clean rags, overlapping them in the same direction as the wheel turns.

29. With the wheelhead spinning slowly, place the plate on the chuck.

30. Center the plate by holding it with both hands and pushing and letting go until it is sitting right.

31. Mark out a circle in the base of the plate with a potter's needle to make sure the plate is properly centered.

32. Use a round turning tool to remove the excess clay from around the base. Check to see that the outer contour matches the inner one.

33. With the triangular turning tool, clean and smooth the base of the plate.

34. You can also use a rectangular rib instead of the turning tool to clean and smooth the base.

35. With the wheel at a standstill, remove the plate and place it back on the chuck, centered and right side up so you can turn the inside.

36. Using a round turning tool so as not to leave any traces, go over the inside of the plate. Hold the tool in the right hand and rest it on the left thumb while the left hand holds the plate.

37 and 38. With the semicircular rib, finish off the inside of the plate. Note how the hands are touching.

39 and 40. Once the interior is finished, turn the plate upside down again, centering it on the chuck, and remove excess clay from around the base with the triangular turning tool.

41. With the same tool, mark the outer ring of the base and shave away the excess clay.

42. Round off the outer edge with a semicircular rib.

43. With the triangular turning tool again, mark the inner part of the ring around the base.

44. Remove the excess clay from the inner base area.

45. Smooth and round off the edge of the ring, and bevel both the outer and inner edge of the ring.

46. With a rib, smooth off the inner base area.

47. The plate is now finished. Do not allow it to dry too quickly or the base could crack. If you have turned at least two plates, you can place them together facing each other (one plate facing up and another inverted on top of it) to prevent warping.

THROWING A CYLINDRICAL POT

A cylindrical pot is the basic piece from which a vase is made. This piece must be mastered before a vase can be thrown successfully. The procedure is the same: knead the clay well, center it, open it, and raise it.

These pieces are generally high and have straight walls. They start off with a truncated cone shape and must be made cylindrical during throwing. It is important that the wall be of equal thickness everywhere. This can be achieved through successive throwing using the knuckles to widen the pot and draw the clay upward, while thinning the walls. This is not an easy task, since the centrifugal force tends to open the clay at the top; this must be counteracted by applying pressure from the outside to maintain the verticality of the walls. During the practice stage, until you can achieve a uniform thickness, you can cut the cylinder vertically to check the evenness of the walls. For this exercise, stoneware clay with fine grog was used, thrown on a wooden bat fitted to the wheelhead.

1. The legs of the bat fit into holes that have been drilled in the wheelhead.

2. Place seven small balls of clay on the wheelhead to absorb any vibrations and keep the bat turning smoothly.

3. Moisten the contact zones of the balls with a damp sponge to ensure a secure adhesion to the bat.

4. Once the bat is put in place, pound it gently in the center to make certain it is attached.

5. Place the kneaded lump of clay on the bat.

6 and 7. Center the lump of clay that is to become a cylindrical pot.

8. Begin opening the clay, but for this exercise make the opening deeper and wider.

9. With your right index finger and left thumb, continue opening the clay.

10. Place your left fingers inside the opening, except the thumb, which should rest on the base of the right palm. With your right hand on the outside to counterbalance and control the pressure, push out with the left hand to widen the opening.

10. Remove your hands to see how deep the opening is.

12. Begin to deepen the opening. Close your right hand and use the index finger to deepen the hole while controlling the outside with the left hand to prevent the clay from coming off center.

13. Continuing in the previous position, lower your hand deeper into the hole being created, following with your left hand on the outside.

14. Control the rim of the cylinder by curling your right index finger over it and backing it with the middle finger and thumb, which should be touching. Keep the upper part steady with your left thumb. Both thumbs should also be touching.

15. Before beginning the first round of throwing with the knuckles, practice the hand position you will use.

16. With your hands still in the previous position, begin to raise the walls. Curl your right hand slightly and bend your index finger with your thumb. Place the left index finger inside the opening, curled up in your thumb, and let the clay pass between your knuckles.

17. Holding the same position, slowly move your hands upward, pressing evenly to thin and raise the wall. Note that your hands should be together to keep them steady. When throwing with the knuckles, it is important always to keep your hands wet.

18. Control the cylinder with both hands, with your right thumb taking care of the rim.

19. Repeat step 14.

20. As your hands reach the upper part of the cylinder, they should be in this position. Rest the left thumb on the right hand to gain better control.

21. Continue throwing with the knuckles, thinning and raising the wall even more.

22. Use a sponge to remove any water that has seeped to the bottom of the cylinder.

23. Practice the hand position you will use in the next step. Hold the rib firmly, parallel to the index finger of the left hand, with the clay passing between them.

24. Holding the rib perpendicular to the base as previously practiced, and beginning from the bottom, carry out another round of raising the wall.

25. Shape the cylinder from the inside by pushing the clay outward toward the rib with your left hand.

26. Sometimes when you remove your hand you may bump into the rim and cause a small blemish, as seen here on the left. You can cut off the damaged part with a potter's needle.

27. Position the hands and the needle this way to mark the area to be cut. Rest the tool against the left thumb.

28. Cut off the ruined rim and, without stopping the wheelhead, lift it off with the left hand without touching the piece.

29. With a rib, smooth off the outer part of the rim near the cutting area.

30. If you want to make a small lip protruding outward from the rim, pinch the rim between the left thumb and index finger. Place the right index finger between them to steady the rim, while your middle finger steadies the side of the cylinder under the left thumb. Slightly incline your left fingers to create the lip.

31. With the edge of a semicircular rib, smooth the outer part of the lip.

32. With a rectangular rib, clean the bat and slightly bevel the edge of the base.

33. The throwing is finished. With the wheel at a standstill, cut under the base with a nylon cutting wire. Remove the bat without touching the cylinder on it, and let the piece dry without disturbing it.

34 and 35. Cylindrical pieces are easy to turn, since clay must be removed only from the base; no clay need be removed from the outer wall, which only requires smoothing. The piece should have taken on a perfectly cylindrical shape during throwing. After drying, the upper wall shrinks slightly and the piece therefore acquires somewhat of a truncated cone shape. If you turn it to try to correct this, when this dries the shrinkage will occur at the lower part. To turn a cylindrical pot, a cylindrical chuck must be used. It should be centered on the wheelhead.

36. Wipe a damp sponge over the centered clay to remove slip.

37. Stop the wheel and place a rag around the cylindrical chuck, trying to keep it smooth and wrinkle-free.

38. Lift the cylinder at the base in both hands and place

it, upside down, on the chuck with the wheelhead in motion.

39. With your hands in the same position, hold the moving piece, letting it spin between your hands. It is also possible to center the piece with the wheel stopped.

40. Place your left hand on the base, pressing slightly, so that the cylinder remains steady. Hold a rectangular rib in your right hand and place it vertically against the lower wall to remove excess clay.

41. With a triangular turning tool, bevel the edge of the base.

42. With the same tool, mark the area to be hollowed.

43 to 45. Using a turning tool, remove clay, hollowing out the base little by little. Repeat the operation until the desired thickness is obtained.

46. Go over the area once more to finish it off.

47. Smooth the inner part of the base with a rectangular rib.

48. Bevel the inner edge of the ring around the base. This beveling will serve to separate the glaze.

49. Go over the outside of the cylinder with a rectangular rib.

50. With the flat side of a semicircular rib, smooth off the outer wall.

51. Once the turning is done, place the piece on a clean surface to dry. As it dries, it will become slightly conical in shape, a defect that will disappear when the piece is completely dry.

THROWING A VASE

Throwing a vase requires some degree of proficiency on the wheel because it is one of the most complex pieces to throw, especially a large one, and large amounts of clay or ceramic body must be handled. During throwing, as the piece becomes higher and wider, it is important to reduce the velocity of the wheel to be able to control the process better. The demonstration that begins on page 54 shows how to throw larger vases using another technique. Red earthenware was used for this vase, which was made directly on the wheelhead without a bat. This process will utilize all the hand positions necessary to make any type of vase.

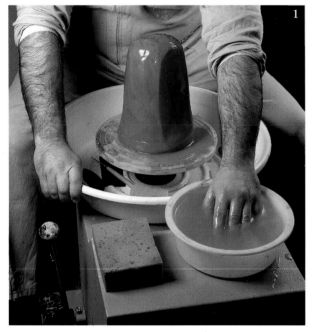

1. Place the prepared clay on the wheelhead, pounding it hard to make sure it is attached. Both the mass of clay and the hands should be moistened with water.

2. Place your right hand on the top of the clay and your left one a bit lower, pressing inward with both hands to center the clay.

3. Once it is centered, place your hands on the upper part of the truncated cone you have shaped and go over the top of it with your thumbs. Dig in with your right thumb to open the clay.

4. With your right index finger and left thumb, widen the opening until it is big enough for one hand to fit in it.

5. Cross both hands to form a V shape and place them inside the opening with your thumbs on the outside. The hands should form a sturdy unit so that when the opening is widened, it doesn't come off center.

6. Once the clay is open, drizzle some water inside for lubrication.

7. Place your right hand on the outside and your left fingers inside the opening, except the thumb, which should rest on the base of the right palm to steady the hands. Push outward with your left hand while controlling the pressure from the outside with the right.

8. Place your right fist inside the opening and use the left hand to control the outside and the rim.

9. As you lower the opening with your right hand, follow with the left to keep the piece centered. With this motion, begin to shape the base cylinder.

10. To control the cylinder, let the rim pass between your right index finger and your thumb

and middle fingers, with both thumbs touching, and control the rim with your left index finger.

11 and 12. Throw a round with your knuckles. Push your hands against the piece, thinning and raising the walls as they rise.

13. Throw another round with your knuckles to thin the walls more and raise the cylinder.

14. Repeat step 10.

15. Wet your hands and slide them gently along the surface of the piece to lubricate it.

16. Place your left hand inside the piece and push outward. The vase will begin to take form. Control the pressure with your right index finger. Throw another round with the knuckles, slowly raising the hands along the wall.

17. Before reaching the upper part, move up your left thumb and rest it on the back of your right hand so the hands form a unit, allowing you more control over this part of the vase.

18. With a semicircular rib, repeat the previous step to refine the exterior surface while shaping the piece.

19. If the rim becomes damaged when removing your hands, use the potter's needle to cut off the damaged top edge.

20. Lift off the cut strip with your left index finger and thumb, making sure it doesn't touch the rim.

21. Place your fingers in a V shape again, controlling the rim as well as beginning to shape what will become the neck.

22. Throw a short round with your knuckles to raise the neck.

23. Narrow the neck a bit by pushing with your thumbs.

24. With the curved edge of a semicircular rib, go over the neck.

25. With the same rib placed obliquely, remove slip from the surface of the vase.

26. With a nylon cutting wire, cut under the vase along the wheelhead to disengage the piece.

27. With clean, dry hands, place the finished vase on a wooden bat and leave it there to dry until it is leather-hard. At this stage turning can begin.

28. Prepare a second lump of clay and make a chuck for turning the vase.

29. With the wheel stopped, hold the vase over the chuck to make sure it fits.

30 and 31. Cover the top of the chuck with rags overlapping in the direction the wheel turns.

32. Place the piece on the chuck and put the wheel in motion. You can also place the piece on the chuck with the wheel spinning slowly. In either case, the piece must be centered. Let it spin between your hands, pressing here and there until it seems perfectly centered.

33. Check to see if the vase is properly centered by drawing a circle on the base with a potter's needle.

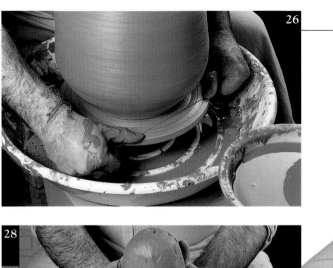

34. Hold a sharp round turning tool firmly with your index finger along the handle so it doesn't wobble. To control the piece and the tool, place your left hand on the upper side of the vase with the thumb touching the right hand. Press the turning tool diagonally into the clay and shave some away. Finish turning the walls of the vase and prepare to do the base.

35. Lower the tool along the surface of the vase. Note the position of the left hand, which holds the base of the piece and touches the turning tool. The lower right arm is held at a right angle with the upper arm against the side of the body, providing greater stability and control when using the turning tool.

36. Make sure the vase is still centered and change tools. To turn the base, it is best to work with a triangular turning tool.

37. Go over the surface of the vase with a rectangular rib.

38. Rest the tool along the line where the base should start and remove 3/8 inch (1 cm) of clay.

39. Continue removing clay from around the base.

40. Bevel the edge of the base slightly with a turning tool.

41. With the same tool, make an incision on the inner part of the base.

42. Remove the excess clay from the inner section.

43. Stop the wheel and tap the base lightly with your finger. With experience, you will be able to judge the thickness of the base from the sound produced.

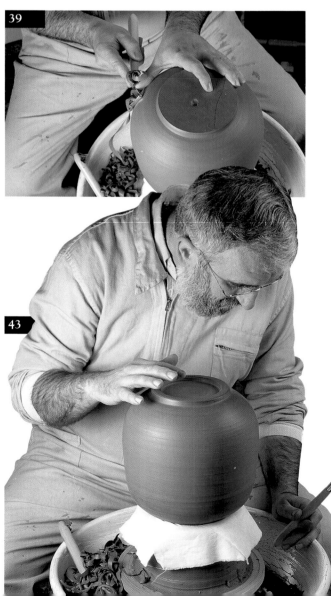

44. Once the ring around the base is finished, bevel the inner edge of the ring as with the outer edge.

45. With the round edge of a semicircular rib, round off the outer edge of the ring.

46 and 47. Go over the surface of the vase with the same rib to smooth and refine it.

48. Remove the neck of the vase from the chuck and check if the base fits in it.

49 and 50. If the base is wider than the mouth of the chuck, you will have to widen the chuck. Stop the wheel, remove the rags, and widen the opening. Clean out the inside with a damp sponge.

51. Replace the rags, place the vase on the chuck, and center it.

52 and 53. With the semicircular rib, go over the neck to smooth it.

54. Stop the wheel and remove the vase from the chuck with clean, dry hands.

55. The turning process is now finished. Place the vase on a flat piece of wood or a rack to dry.

FORMING SPOUTS

Throwing pieces with spouts begins with a cylindrical form that is transformed and elongated so that any liquid that will be poured with it does not drip. Spouts can also be thrown separately, starting with balls of clay or other ceramic body, or from a lump of clay. Until you acquire experience, it may be necessary to make at least two per piece before you create a good one. The spout should be added when the clay reaches the leather-hard state.

If you are making a spout as part of the original piece, it should be done immediately after throwing the piece.

1. Begin with a cylinder of prepared clay.

2. Make the cylinder as thin and high as possible from the inside, then from the outside, using both index fingers and both thumbs.

3. To give it its final shape, use the edge of a semicircular rib.

4. A spout can also be thrown from a lump of clay just as if making a small pot.

5. After shaping it, mark the cutting line on it with a potter's needle or with the fingernail of your left thumb. Cut it with a silk cutting wire.

6. Another type of spout can be made from a small cylinder of clay.

7. With a nylon cutting wire, cut off a small section from the top the cylinder.

8. Place it on the form that will become a jug. Let both parts

become hard and then join them, first with slip and then by adding a coil of the same clay as used for the jug for reinforcement. Then cut out the part of the jug covered by the base of the spout and use it to reinforce the inner join.

9. Another option is to make the spout directly on the thrown jug. Place your left thumb and index finger perpendicular to the rim of the jug, reaching down from above. With the index finger of your right hand, pull the rim outward between the other fingers. The two left fingers keep the rest of the rim from deforming.

10. This is a spout made with the method in step 9.

FORMING HANDLES AND KNOBS

*H*andles and knobs can be made using different methods. They can be modeled as well as thrown. But they must have one thing in common: they must fit the piece in form as well as function. Both handles and knobs are attached to the piece in a leather-hard state.

1. To throw a handle from a cylinder of clay, shape the cylinder between your left index finger and thumb. At the same time, draw a line with your right middle finger to mark the cutting line and control the upper edge with the right index finger.

2. Holding the cylinder from the inside with the fingers of your left hand, rest a potter's needle on the left thumb and cut the handle from the cylinder.

3. After cutting it, lift the handle without deforming it

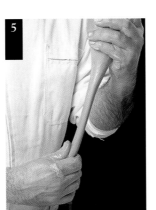

and place it somewhere to dry before attaching it to the piece.

4. Another method of preparing handles, the pulling technique, uses a kneaded ceramic body of homogenous consistency. Prepare a ball of clay and hold it in your left hand. Wet your right hand, form a ring with the index finger and the thumb, and place it on top of the ball of clay. Push downward, making the ring smaller as you descend. Repeat this procedure until you achieve the desired thickness and length. The hand should be lubricated before every repetition.

5. Continue to pull the clay and then flatten it by rubbing your thumb over the surface.

6. Curve it into shape and let it harden.

7. Cut off the extra clay at the ball side.

8. Place your left thumb on the upper part of a prepared lump of

clay, with your left index and middle fingers on the side, while the knob is shaped with your right index and middle fingers.

9. With the fingernail of your right thumb, mark the cutting line.

10. Cut off the knob with a cutting wire.

11. This hand position also works for shaping a knob.

12. The knob is ready for cutting.

13. This knob was prepared the same way as the one in step 11, except that it is shaped with the round edge of a semicircular rib.

14. A potter's needle can also be used to trace the cutting line.

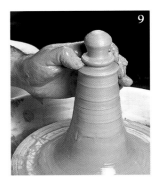

FORMING LIDS

*S*ome thrown pieces including casseroles, pots, soup tureens, and teapots require a lid. The lid and the main piece should form a whole. The shape of the rim on a piece will determine the type of lid. This exercise illustrates the procedure for throwing a lid of the exact diameter to fit either the interior or exterior lip, depending on the piece.

Just as with the spouts, it is a good idea to throw two lids for each piece at first, until you feel you have mastered the technique. The lid should be put in place after both it and the piece have been turned, so that complete the drying process together and do not warp. They should also be fired together.

Types of Lids

Two types of lids can be thrown: those that are thrown right side up, and those thrown upside down. The former are thrown together with the knob and should not need to be turned unless they require a flange.

When throwing the latter type, you can either figure in the additional clay for the knob, or you can add it after turning. Both methods are correct, so choose the one most convenient for you according to the shape of the lid. Some lids have a flange to hold them in place on the piece, while others won't need one because the piece itself will be thrown with a flange on its rim to hold up the lid.

Throwing a Lid Right Side

1. Center a prepared lump of clay and use your thumbnail to mark the amount of clay you think necessary.

2. Holding the clay with your left hand, throw with the fingers of your right. With the middle finger, apply inward pressure to shape the lid, controlling the upper part with the index finger and the lower part with the ring finger.

3. As the knob begins to form, move the fingers of both hands as a unit to avoid moving the clay off center.

4. Maintaining the same position, finish throwing the knob with the tips of your fingers.

5 and 6. Prepare another lid with the same lump of clay. The same procedure will be used, except this time it will be shaped like a bowl. Pinch the clay between your left index finger and thumb while controlling the rim and the lower part of the lid with the index and middle fingers of your right hand. Note how the hands are held together, working as a unit to avoid shifting the piece off-center.

7. With a rib, smooth the surface and mark out the cutting line.

8. The lid can also be thrown from a ball of clay on a wooden bat to avoid warping.

9. Center the ball of clay in the marked position. As in the previous steps for throwing lids, the fingertips are used. Once the ball has been centered, control the diameter with the middle, ring, and pinkie fingers of your left hand, as well as with your right ring and pinkie fingers. At the same time, push in toward the middle with your left thumb and right index and middle fingers to form the knob.

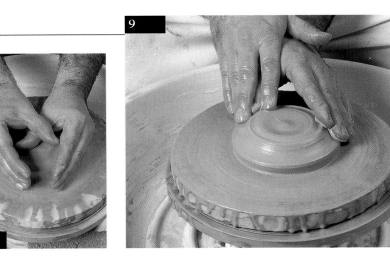

10. Your hands should be in this position when shaping the knob.

11. Continue to pinch the sides of the knob to thin and raise it.

12. Cut of the top of the knob with a potter's needle.

13. The thrown lid with flange is finished.

Throwing a Lid Upside Down

1. Begin to throw a bowl shape, opening the lump of clay with your left thumb and right index finger.

2. Make the lip and flange of the lid by pinching the outer rim between your left index finger and thumb and the inner one between your right index finger and thumb.

3. Smooth the lip and flange with a rib.

4. Another type of upside down lid can be made from a ball of clay centered on a wooden bat.

5. Open up the lump by pulling outward with your right index finger and left thumb.

6. Raise the wall, pinching it between your left index finger and thumb while keeping it centered with the side of your right hand.

7 to 9. With a rectangular rib, go over the inside, outside, and rim of the lid.

10. Check the inner diameter with a curved compass.

Turning a Lid

1. Prepare a chuck in the shape of a truncated cone for turning. Cover it with rags and place the lid on it in a centered position. In this case, place the lid with the knob underneath, inside the chuck. Bevel the rim, then use a turning tool to hollow out the inner lid.

2. The finished lid should look something like this.

3. After turning a bowl-shaped lid, round the outer surface with a triangular turning tool.

4. Using the potter's needle, score the center, add slip, and place a small ball of clay on it.

5. Throw the knob as explained in the corresponding section above.

6. The finished lid with knob should look something like this.

THROWING A JUG

Jugs are meant to hold as well as pour liquids. They have three basic components: the body, the spout, and the handle. Each one serves a different purpose. The body contains the liquid, the spout pours the liquid without spilling it, and the handle, strong enough to hold the weight of the jug as well as the liquid in it, allows for comfort in holding the jug while pouring.

For this piece, a kneaded lump of red earthenware was prepared and thrown as if for a vase. Its shape is typical for these pieces. In this case, turning is not necessary afterward, but if it were necessary, it would be done according to the steps explained for the cylindrical pot (pages 34-35). Remember that the handle should only be added after turning.

5. Prepare a ball of clay to make the handle using the pulling technique.

6. Cut the pulled handle to the appropriate length and join it to the jug opposite the spout. Before joining it, score the surfaces to be joined with a needle and add slip as reinforcement.

7. Holding the jug by the base in your left hand, finish pulling the handle with your right hand (be sure your hand is lubricated with water). Then bend the handle and join it to the lower wall, then touch up the joins.

8. All pieces with a handle should be dried slowly. The jug should not be lifted by the handle until it has been bisque-fired.

1. Center a lump of clay on a wooden bat placed on the wheelhead. Proceed to open the lump as explained in previous sections.

2. Use the knuckles to throw the base cylinder.

3. Shape the lower part of the jug. Go over the outer wall with a rib to remove slip and then refine the rim between your fingers.

4. To form the spout, place your left thumb and index finger at an angle on the outer rim of the jug, and your right index finger on the inner rim between them. For this procedure, your fingers must be well lubricated with slip. Pull the rim outward with your right index finger to make the spout. Pass a cutting wire under the jug to separate it from the bat, but leave it in place to harden so it does not become misshapen.

THROWING A TEAPOT

*T*he teapot, one of the most complicated exercises in this book, is made up of four parts: the body, the lid, the spout, and the handle. Form follows function for each part. The same concept of functionality implies that the teapot should not be heavy, since it will contain liquid. The spout must be placed at a certain height so that the teapot can be filled to the brim. The lid is thrown here along with the body, to demonstrate yet another way of making a lid. The handle should be strong enough to hold the weight of the pot, but also comfortable to grip and placed so as to facilitate pouring. It can be placed opposite the spout or on the upper part of the teapot. The entire piece should form an aesthetically as well as a functionally harmonious whole.

Each part should be thrown separately and joined once the pieces are leather-hard. Although all the elements can be thrown, in this case the handle will be pulled. Stoneware was used for the teapot in this exercise.

1. Place the prepared lump of clay on a wooden disc attached to the wheelhead. Slowly give it the appropriate shape and begin to thin the neck.

2. Continue to thin the neck, and then remove slip from the surface with a rectangular rib.

3. The neck should be thinned until it is almost closed up.

4. With both thumbs and index fingers, press inward to close the opening completely.

5. Shape the knob by placing your left thumb and middle finger at the base and your index finger on the upper part, with your right pinkie at the base.

6. Finish shaping it using your left thumb and right and left index and middle fingers. Scrape the surface with a rib to clean it. The air trapped inside the piece keeps it from deforming.

7. After the piece has been turned, mark out the lid and cut it at an oblique angle with a sharp potter's needle.

8. Use a turning tool to adjust the underside of the lid.

9. Once the teapot is shaped you may want to make several different spouts to try out various looks.

10. Cut the chosen spout at an angle to fit the side of the teapot. It may take several cuts before you achieve a good fit. Hold the spout against the body and mark its outline with a potter's needle. Remove the spout and use the drill to make holes inside the marked circle. Score the surfaces to be joined and lubricate them with slip.

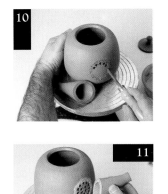

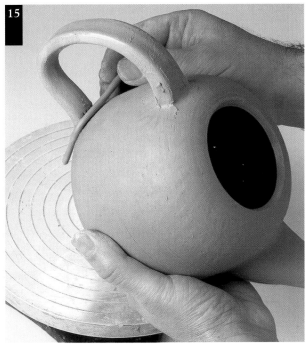

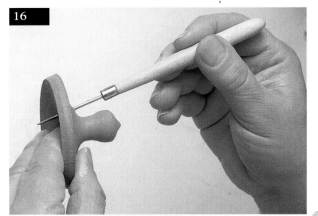

11 and 12. Fit the two parts together and hold them until they are well joined. Score around the join with the needle.

13. Place a small roll of clay along the scored join and press it with a modeling tool to meld the parts.

14 and 15. Pull and cut a handle (see page 43) and place it on the side of the teapot opposite the spout. Join the handle and reinforce the joins with small rolls of clay, as with the spout.

16. To prevent condensation from forming inside the lid, make a small hole from the outside with a potter's needle.

17. The finished teapot should dry slowly in a safe place. Cover the handle with a piece of plastic to keep it from breaking. The lid should remain in place during drying and firing.

THROWING A BOWL WITH A CYLINDRICAL BASE

*T*o make a bowl with a base, it is best to throw two separate pieces. It's possible to throw it as a single piece, but the upper part will be narrower and may cave in if you widen it. Throwing two separate pieces is more practical. You can also make the base out of a hol-low cone of clay, like a tube. In this case, it should be attached both on the inside and the outside to reinforce the join. When varnishing the piece, the join should be varnished as well for additional reinforcement. This piece was made with stoneware containing fine grog.

1. Place seven small balls of clay on the wheelhead to act as shock absorbers and place a wooden bat on top (the clay balls will keep it from vibrating). Pound the center of the bat with your fist to make it stay in place. Spread some clay over the bat so that the lump of clay to be worked sticks better. Center the prepared lump of clay for the bowl part of the piece.

2. With your right thumb, begin opening the clay. Widen the opening with your right index finger and left thumb.

3. Begin to deepen the opening using all your fingers. The opening will become wider.

4. Place your left fingers inside the opening and pull outward to make it still wider. From the outside, control the rim with your left thumb and the wall with your right hand.

5. Begin to shape the bowl with your knuckles. Refine the rim with both hands to maintain the centering.

6 and 7. Repeat step 5 twice to increase the bowl's size.

8. Go over the outer surface of the bowl with the semicircular rib to finish it off. Remove the bat with the thrown bowl and leave it to be turned later.

9. Center another lump of clay on another bat and begin to throw the base. It will have a truncated cone shape.

10. Open the clay following step 3 above. Controlling the rim, begin deepening the opening with your right fist on the inside and your left hand counterbalancing on the outside.

11. Use your knuckles to raise and thin the walls. As you reach the rim, take your thumb from inside and rest it on the back of your other hand to steady it.

12. Lubricate the cylinder with water and slip. Begin a second round of throwing with the knuckles to give the base its final shape.

13. Refine the outer surface with the rectangular rib. As you reach the rim, take out your thumb again and rest it on the rib to keep it under control.

14. Take the rim between your right index and middle fingers and bend it outward to form a lip.

15. Using the round part of the semicircular rib, finish off and refine the upper part of the base.

16. Refine the rim by pinching it between your fingers and running your right index finger along the top.

17. Cut the bat away from the base with a nylon cutting wire and remove the bat, leaving the piece in place on top. Set it aside to dry.

18. When both parts reach the leather-hard state, they are ready to be turned.

19. Prepare a conical chuck and cover it with rags. Invert the base piece and center it on the chuck. Remove excess clay with a rounded turning tool.

20 and 21. With a triangular turning tool, bevel the bottom edge of the base. Then trace an inner circle on the bottom and remove extra clay to hollow it out a bit. Smooth it with a rectangular rib.

22. Open out the chuck so it fits the bowl, and then center the inverted bowl on it.

23. Remove excess clay around the outside base of the bowl with a round turning tool. Then go over it with the semicircular rib.

24 and 25. With the potter's needle, mark a circle of equal diameter to the inside edge of the base piece. Make more circles outside the first one to insure a better join.

26. Score the area to be joined with the needle and moisten it with a sponge.

27 and 28. Score the rim of the base piece and moisten it with slip.

29. Add slip to the scored area of the bowl and lower the base onto it. With the wheelhead spinning very slowly, center the base on the bowl, guided by the circles marked earlier.

30. Score the join to reinforce it.

31 and 32. Place a small roll of clay around the join and press it in place with a wooden tool, spreading it up the bowl sides and onto the base.

32. With the semicircular rib, smooth and round off the surface.

34. With the potter's needle, make a hole on the underside of the base to allow air trapped inside to escape.

35. The finished piece should look something like this.

THROWING A VASE IN TWO PARTS

*T*hrowing a large piece requires some mastery of the wheel. It is easier to create in two or three parts, rather than one. In this exercise it is done in two parts. It is important to have wooden bats with feet to anchor them into the wheelhead. This procedure is useful for throwing large or tall pieces of thin or regular diameter. For large pieces of wide diameter, it is best to use the technique of throwing with coils; in that case the base is made first, then each coil is thrown separately and allowed to harden between each throwing.

This piece was made with stoneware containing fine grog. First throw a truncated cone shape for the upper part of the vase, then throw the base piece separately. Both follow the same general procedure.

1. Place the clay on a wooden bat, wet it abundantly, and begin centering it.

2 and 3. Center the clay and begin opening it.

4 and 5. Deepen the hole and raise the walls to form a cylinder.

6. Throw a round with your knuckles to thin and raise the walls.

7. Score the rim with a potter's needle.

8. Throw the other piece in the same way, following the shape seen here. Be sure the two openings have the same diameter so they can be joined properly.

9. Transport the upper part by handling the bat, which will prevent having to touch it and risk deforming it. Place it, inverted, on top of the base piece.

10. With a nylon cutting wire, separate the upper piece from the bat and make a hole with a potter's needle big enough to fit your hand through.

11. Join the two pieces and throw a round with your knuckles just beneath the join to make a truncated cone shape. Smooth the surface with a rectangular rib.

12. Cut off the top with the needle to even the surface. With a sponge, remove any water that may have accumulated inside the vase.

13. Continue to throw and raise the vase and thin the walls, throwing several rounds with your knuckles. Then smooth the rim as shown.

14 and 15. Narrow and elongate the neck of the vase, positioning the hands as shown. Smooth it off with the rounded edge of a rib.

16. Pinch the rim and refine it. Go over the entire surface to remove traces of slip. The throwing is complete.

17. When the vase has reached the leather-hard state, return the bat to the wheel and go over the vase surface with a curved rib.

18 and 19. Refine the surface with the rectangular and then the semicircular rib.

20. Use a steel wire to separate the vase from the bat.

21. To prepare the chuck on which to turn the base of the piece, place a well-kneaded

lump of clay on the wheel-head and another on top of that.

22 and 23. Center the two lumps as if they were one and begin opening the chuck.

24. When the chuck is finished, cover it with rags and prepare a long string with a knot at each end. Embed one end into the chuck under the rags.

25 and 26. Let the wheel turn slowly while winding the string up the side of the chuck and back down again. Embed the other knot into the chuck. The string will keep the chuck from falling apart from the weight of the vase.

27. Place the inverted vase in the chuck and center it.

28 and 29. First with the round turning tool and then with the triangular one, remove excess clay.

30 and 31. With the round turning tool, shave off clay to form a more pronounced base around the ring and bevel the edge of the ring. Do the same with the triangular turning tool around the inside of the ring.

32. The finished vase should look something like this.

"NERIAGE" VASE

*N*eriage is a decorative technique involving mixing two or more clay bodies that are of naturally different colors or are colored with metal oxides. It is best to use types of clay that have the same shrinkage rate to prevent crackling during the drying or firing stages, unless this is a desired artistic effect. The procedure that is explained here presents no problems since only a single type of ceramic body, part of it colored with cobalt oxide (CoO), is used. Coloring can be done with any of the usual metal oxides. Be careful about the quantity of oxide mixed in, since too much of it can create bubbles and can lower the melting point of the clay.

1. You will need two lumps of porcelain in a semidry state and a mallet.

2 and 3. With the mallet, break up one of the lumps into small pieces.

4. Place a clean cloth on a drying rack and lay out the bits of porcelain. Allow them to dry out completely.

5. Once dry, continue breaking them down until

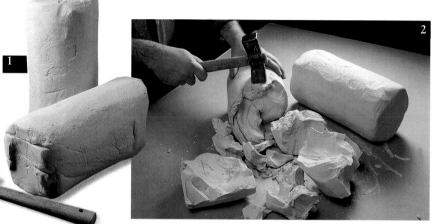

the pieces are about 9/16 inch (1.5 cm) in diameter.

6. Grind the bits with a rolling pin until they almost reach the powder state.

7. Weigh 1 kg of powdered clay body on a scale. Prepare a total of 4 piles of powdered clay, each 1 kg.

8. Weigh 1 percent, then 3 percent, then 6 percent cobalt oxide on a precision scale.

9. With a mortar and pestle, mix the separate piles of powdered clay with the oxide. First add a bit of clay to the mortar, then mix in the oxide, then more powdered clay until a uniform color is produced. Mix the other piles the same way with the other strengths of oxide.

10. The uncolored clay powder is seen at the upper left, followed by the mixed piles (moving clockwise) of 1, 3, and 6 percent. The cobalt oxide is at lower left.

11. Pour 800 cc of water into a clean plastic container and sprinkle one pile of colored porcelain powder into it by hand. Mix it and let it soak for at least 48 hours, then spill out the water that has accumulated over the clay.

12. Prepare the other three powders the same way.

13. Cover a dry slab of plaster with a clean cloth to prevent

particles of plaster from mixing in with the clay. Make a simple stand with four blocks of wood around the plaster and place a stainless steel sieve (grade 49) on top. Using gloves and a plastic spatula, sift the moist uncolored clay through the sieve.

14. Spread the sifted clay on the plaster slab to a thickness of about 2 inches (5 cm). Repeat with the other shades.

15. This clay was left to dry for four days. It was then kneaded and allowed to rest for a month before using it.

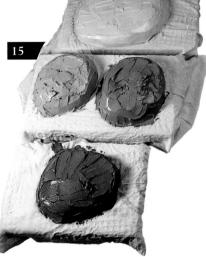

16. Knead all the clay in preparation for throwing. Place the three lumps of colored clay around the uncolored one.

17. Knead them slightly into one large lump.

18. Place a wooden bat on the wheelhead and add the lump of clay to throw a large vase.

19. Center the clay. The entire mass of clay appears colored, but the color is only on the surface.

20. Begin opening the centered clay with both hands.

21. With your left hand supporting the outside, deepen the opening with your right fist until the base reaches the appropriate thickness.

22. Raise the cylinder by throwing a round with your knuckles. The walls will become thinner as they rise.

23. Smooth the exterior wall with a rib while controlling the inside with your left hand.

24. Shape the vase by pressing outward with your left hand. Use both hands to make the neck a bit narrower.

25. Shape the neck with the round edge of a semicircular rib. Hold the rib in the right hand and rest it against the left thumb.

26. To narrow the neck, let it pass between your right index and middle fingers while pushing with your left hand. Squeeze it with the fingers of both hands to narrow it further. Note how the left index finger controls the rim of the neck. Remove excess slip by going over the surface with a rib placed at an angle.

27. The throwing process is finished. Slide a cutting wire under the base to disengage the vase from the wheel. Let the piece harden until it reaches the leather-hard state.

28. Prepare the chuck and cover it with rags. Place the inverted vase on the chuck.

29. With the wheel spinning slowly, center the vase by pushing gently with both hands.

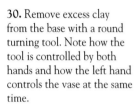

30. Remove excess clay from the base with a round turning tool. Note how the tool is controlled by both hands and how the left hand controls the vase at the same time.

31. Continue removing clay, slowly moving downward.

32 and 33. Continue removing excess clay from the base toward the chuck.

34. Smooth the entire vase with a rectangular rib.

35. Remove the vase from the chuck and turn it over to finish off the neck.

36. Refine the neck with a triangular turning tool.

37. With the same turning tool, remove clay from the lower part to the upper.

38. With the same turning tool, work on the circumference of the base.

39. With the tip of a semicircular rib, round off the outer part of the base and bevel the edge of the inner base.

40 and 41. With a triangular turning tool, remove excess clay from the center of the base and then bevel the inner edge of the ring you have made on the base.

42. Stop the wheel and with clean, dry hands, remove the vase from the chuck. Note how clean the lines of color are.

43. After bisque-firing the vase looks paler.

44. Varnishing brings out the richness of the colors.

Chavarria.
Sinfonía en azul. 1987.
$7^{1}/_{2} \times 7^{1}/_{2}$ in. (19 × 19 cm)
Firing temperature: 2336°F (1280°C).

GLOSSARY

Aging. Process of placing clay aside after kneading to allow it to acquire greater plasticity.

Air bubbles. Masses of air trapped in clay or other ceramic body that will cause cracks or breakage during drying or firing. They can also be found in plaster.

Airing. Process of allowing the clay to air out to eliminate some of the moisture content.

Bat. Disk made of wood, plaster of paris, or fired clay, placed on the wheelhead to provide a larger working surface or one that can be moved without handling the thrown piece directly.

Beveling. Cutting the edge of a piece of clay at a slanting angle.

Capillary action. The process, caused by surface tension, by which water is drawn to the surface through microscopic tubes in the clay body. Once at the surface, the water evaporates.

Cavity. A hole in the interior of a mass of clay or other ceramic body.

Centrifugal force. Force acting upon pieces being thrown on the wheel, which tends to send them outward, away from the center.

Chemically combined water. Water that is chemically combined with clay.

Clay body. A mixture of various types of clay with minerals and other nonplastic materials.

Collapse. When a piece caves in due to its own weight.

Contraction. Shrinkage.

Firing. Heating a clay piece to a specific temperature to mature it.

Flange. The upper part of a jar or other piece into which the lid fits, or the part of the lid that fits into a jar, teapot, or the like.

Foot. Base existing on some thrown pieces.

Grog. Bisque-fired, ground clay. Grog can be coarse-grained, fine, or very fine.

Harmonious. Well proportioned.

Joining. Uniting clay or ceramic body surfaces with slip.

Kneading. Manipulating a mass of clay with the hands until it reaches a homogenous consistency.

Leather-hard. State of clay that is partially dry but still retains some moisture. Pieces thrown on the wheel are later turned in this state.

Lip. Part of a jug or vase that holds the lid (i.e., the rim), or the part of the lid that rests on the lip of the piece.

Lubricating. Wetting hands and the piece with water or slip during throwing to avoid sticking.

Lump. Mass of clay or other ceramic body that is kneaded and ready to throw.

Melamine. Plastic coating on a board that forms a good working surface.

Modeling. Additive process by which the piece is enhanced with the addition of soft materials such as clay.

Mortar. Bowllike container in which ceramic materials are mixed or ground, generally with a pestle.

Overlapping. Method of placing rags on a chuck so that they do not curl up at the edges. The rags should overlap in the direction the wheel spins.

Pivot. Wooden or metallic cylinder fit into a base and on which the manual potter's wheel turns.

Plaster. A composition of various materials such as lime, gypsum, sand, and water.

Plaster slab. Used to absorb excess moisture from clay or other ceramic body.

Plasticity. Property of clay that allows it to hold the shape given it when modeling.

Pottery. Ceramic ware, including thrown pieces.

Precision scale. Precision balance for taking very fine measurements or weighing small amounts.

Rags. Pieces of cotton cloth placed on the chuck for the turning process so the thrown piece will not stick to the chuck.

Raw piece. Piece before firing.

Scoring. Tracing lines with a needle on two pieces to strengthen a join before covering them with slip.

Shoulder. Part of a jug or vase next to the lip.

Shrinkage. Contraction of the clay during drying and firing.

Sieve. Tool for sifting material in the liquid, powder, or paste state.

Slip. Watery clay mixture used to join parts of a piece when they are in a leather-hard state.

Soaking. Softening clay or ceramic body with water.

Turning. Process of removing surplus clay on thrown pieces in the leather-hard state to smooth and refine the surface.

Wheelhead. The flat disk located on top of the wheel axis on which pieces are thrown.